THATCH

VOICES FROM THE TRADITIONAL HOUSES OF COUNTY LAOIS

MARY ANN WILLIAMS

SINÉAD HUGHES AND BRONAGH LANIGAN

featuring

Photography by James Fraher and Alf Harvey

Illustrations by Máirtín D'Alton

PUBLISHED BY LAOIS COUNTY COUNCIL WITH THE SUPPORT OF THE HERITAGE COUNCIL

2011

© Laois County Council 2011

Text © Mary Ann Williams 2011

Illustrations © Máirtín D'Alton, Dip Arch B Arch Sc MLitt MRIAI

Photographs © James Fraher and Alf Harvey unless otherwise indicated

Alf Harvey: cover, 28, 29 top, 60

James Fraher: frontispiece, contents, 4-7, 11-17, 18 left, 19-27, 29 middle and bottom, 30-31, 34-36, 38 top right, 39 left, 40 top, 41 except inset, 42-43, 45 bottom left, 46 left, 47 top, 50 bottom, 51 top, 52-53, 54 bottom left and bottom right, 56-58, 59 top, 61-63, inside back cover, back cover

This publication is available to purchase from:
Catherine Casey
Heritage Officer
Laois County Council
Portlaoise, Co Laois
Phone 057 867 4348
ccasey@laoiscoco.ie
www.laois.ie/heritage
www.facebook.com/laois.heritage.forum

All rights reserved. This item may not be reproduced in any form or by any means — graphic, electronic or mechanical, including recording, taping or information retrieval systems — without the prior permission in writing of the publishers.

Graphic Design by Connie Scanlon and James Fraher, Bogfire www.bogfire.com

Typeset in Minion and Calibri

Printed in Ireland

ISBN 978-1-899642-09-0

British Library Cataloguing-in-Publication Data

A catalogue record for this book is available from the British Library.

Laois County Council would like to thank the Heritage Council for its support of this publication.

CONTENTS

ACKNOWLEDGEMENTS	4
FOREWORD / BROLLACH	5
INTRODUCTION / RÉAMHRÁ	6
COUNTING HOUSES	8
STRUCTURE	14
Thatching	16
A House of History: Abbeyview Cottage	24
Michael Dempsey	27
HARVEST	28
HOMEPLACE	32
Jimmy Dowling	36
A Happy Family Home: The House at Jamestown Cross	38
The Rarest of Them All: Crannagh House	40
Seamus Conroy	41
A Time Capsule: The House at Clonaghadoo	42
ALL MOD CONS	44
A House of Changes: Mary Bergin's House	46
Jackie Kavanagh	47
BUNGALOW BLISS	48
DEATH OF A HOUSE	49
The House at Pass of the Plumes	49
PUBS AND OTHER THATCHED BUSINESSES	50
THATCH IN A NEW ERA	55
A 21st Century Thatch: Philip and Penny Doran's House	56
Philip Doran	59
CHALLENGES	61
THE LAST WORD	62
ABOUT THE AUTHORS	63
BIBLIOGRAPHY	63
PHOTO INDEX	64

ACKNOWLEDGEMENTS

This book is based on *Survey of Thatched Structures in Laois, 2007*, a report resulting from the intensive fieldwork of Sinéad Hughes and Bronagh Lanigan of Architectural Recording and Research, with the support of Laois County Council and the Heritage Council.

Further details on all aspects of thatch in Laois, including technical reports on the 2007 survey, are available at www.laois.ie/thatch.

The publication was initiated and edited by Catherine Casey, Laois Heritage Officer, and a Steering Group of Laois Heritage Forum. Thanks to Angela McEvoy, Senior Planner, Laois County Council; Anne Goodwin, CEO of Laois Partnership; Dr Jack Carter, Ballyfin and Tom Cox, Abbeyleix Heritage House.

Mary Ann Williams would like to thank Michael, Emily and Patrick Ryan; Emily Huie, Patty Kupicha and Pamela Wallace for their help during this project.

Bronagh Lanigan and Sinéad Hughes would like to acknowledge the help and enthusiasm of Michael Dempsey of Jamestown, Ballybrittas; Críostóir Mac Cárthaigh of the School of Irish, Celtic Studies, Irish Folklore & Linguistics at UCD; and Terry and Frank Mitchell of Mountmellick, who kindly accommodated us during fieldwork.

Thanks to all of the owners of thatched houses, thatchers, those who helped with research and those who shared their experiences, memories and photographs of thatch in Laois.

Lesley Bailey	Michael, Brigid, Oliver and Martin Dempsey	Teddy Fennelly	Julie Lalor	Clare Mulhall
Mary Bergin		Ned Ging (RIP)	Mary Lalor	Margaret McLoughlin Mulhall
Tony Bergin		Kevin Higgins	Tom Lawlor	
Margaret and Pat Brennan	Philip and Penny Doran	Kevin Hogan	Jake Lawlor	Kay Moore
Noel Butler	Jimmy Dowling	Jackie Hyland	Bridie Lewis	Maureen Palmer
Ivor Conroy	Mick Dowling	Maria Hyland	Ronnie Mathews	Nancy Phelan
Seamus Conroy	Eddie Dunne	Jackie Kavanagh	Dolores McEvoy	Tom Treacy
Theresa Delahunty	Mary Dunne	Gertie Keane	Liam and Abigail McEvoy	Sean Ward
P.J. Delaney	Stephen Dunne	Michael Keane	Rena McEvoy	Aisling Ryan

We extend special thanks to the people who gave assistance and insight to this project, but who do not wish to be acknowledged.

Thanks to Maurice O'Keeffe of Irish Life and Lore (www.irishlifeandlore.com) for permission to use material from his 2006 interview with thatcher Seamus Conroy.

Thanks to the National Archives of Ireland and its Director Dr David V. Craig for permission to reproduce the following records: NAI, Census 1911, Queen's County, DED 70/9, form A 6 for the family of James Bates. NAI, Census 1911, Queen's County, DED 70/9, form B 1 for Raheenahoran.

Thanks to Brendan Delany and the ESB Archive for permission to use the advertisements that appear on pages 44-45.

This book was funded by Laois County Council and the Heritage Council under the *Laois Heritage Plan 2007-2011*.

FOREWORD

As Cathaoirleach of Laois County Council, I am delighted to welcome the publication of this book, which celebrates the thatched houses of County Laois and the people who live in and look after them.

This book is an action of the Laois Heritage Plan 2007 – 2011 and follows on from a comprehensive survey of thatch in the county carried out in 2007. Its publication reflects the high priority given to thatch by the public in Laois and the members of the Laois Heritage Forum. I would like to commend the members of the Heritage Forum and in particular our Heritage Officer, Catherine Casey, for their hard work and dedication in commissioning the survey and preparing this book.

The book celebrates both the thatched houses themselves and the people associated with them, past and present. The thatched houses that remain in Laois and throughout Ireland, have, after all, survived because of the love, care and attention of the people in whose care they have been entrusted.

Thatch is an integral part of the architectural heritage of County Laois. This book will help to ensure that thatch will remain relevant into the future. I wish to congratulate the authors for their commitment in researching and writing this valuable addition to the heritage of County Laois. I hope that the publication of this book will raise the profile of thatch in the county, and make the wider public aware of the huge value of these traditional houses in the Irish landscape.

John Bonham, MCC
Cathaoirleach of Laois County Council

BROLLACH

Mar Chathaoirleach ar Chomhairle Chontae Laoise, fáiltím roimh fhoilsiú an leabhair seo ina ndéantar ceiliúradh ar thithe ceann tuí i gContae Laoise agus ar na daoine a chónaíonn iontu agus a thugann aire dóibh.

Leabhar í seo atá curtha i dtoll a chéile ag Plean Oidhreachta Laoise 2007 – 2011 i ndiaidh suirbhé cuimsitheach a déanadh ar thithe ceann tuí in 2007. Léiríonn an foilseachán an tábhacht a bhaineann le tuí do phobal Chontae Laoise agus do bhaill Fhóram Oidhreachta Laoise. Molaim baill an Fhóraim Oidhreachta agus ár nOifigeach Oidhreachta Catherine Casey as an obair chrua a rinne siad agus as a dtiomantas ó thaobh an suirbhé a choimisiúnú agus an leabhar a ullmhú.

Déanann an leabhar ceiliúradh ar na tithe ceann tuí féin agus ar na daoine a raibh ceangal acu leo san am a caitheadh agus orthusan a bhfuil ceangal acu leo san am i láthair. Is mar gheall ar an gcion, an aire agus ar an gcúram a fuair tithe ceann tuí ó na daoine a raibh siad faoina na gcúram a mhair na tithe i gCo. Laoise agus ar fud na hÉireann.

Is cuid lárnach d'oidhreacht sheandálaíochta Chontae Laoise é an tuí. Cuideoidh an leabhar seo lena chinntiú go mbeidh tábhacht ag baint leis an tuí amach anseo. Ba mhaith liom comhghairdeas a dhéanamh leis na húdair as an taighde a rinneadh agus as an leabhar seo a a scríobh, leabhar a chuirfidh go mór le hoidhreacht Chontae Laoise. Tá súil agam go dtarraingeoidh an leabhar seo aird ar an tuí sa chontae agus go gcuirfidh sé an pobal i gcoitinne ar an eolas faoin tábhacht a bhaineann leis na tithe traidisiúnta seo i dtírdhreach na hÉireann.

John Bonham, MCC
Cathaoirleach Chomhairle Chontae Laoise

INTRODUCTION

I am delighted to join with the Cathaoirleach in welcoming the publication of this book on thatch in Laois.

Laois County Council has been proactive in delivering a heritage service for the county, and was one of the first Local Authorities nationally to appoint a full-time Heritage Officer. Through the years since the publication of our first Heritage Plan in 2001, the support of the Heritage Council has been crucial and unwavering. I would like to thank the Board and Staff of the Heritage Council for their commitment to heritage throughout Ireland.

A key finding of the original survey of thatch in Laois was that owners of thatched houses require more support, both in accessing practical information to assist them in the conservation of their houses, and equally importantly, in securing funding to carry out the ongoing work required to keep these houses alive.

Laois County Council has taken an important step in adding many of these houses to our Record of Protected Structures, which will not only give the buildings strong legal protection, but should also allow allow owners to access funding for conservation work, not only to the thatch but also to the other aspects of these houses which add to their historic value, including windows, doors and other original features. I urge all those owners whose houses are now on the Record of Protected Structures to access this funding.

I hope that this book will be enjoyed by all owners of thatched houses, those who have memories of thatch, and anyone with an interest in the heritage of Laois.

Peter Carey
County Manager

RÉAMHRÁ

Tá ríméad ormsa, chomh maith leis an gCathaoirleach, faoi go bhfuil an leabhar seo faoin tuí i gContae Laoise á foilsiú.

Bhí Comhairle Chontae Laoise an-ghníomhach ó thaobh seirbhís oidhreachta a chur ar fáil sa chontae agus bhí sí ar an gcéad údarás áitiúil a cheap Oifigeach Oidhreachta go lánaimseartha. Ó foilsíodh ár gcéad Phlean Oidhreachta in 2001, tá tacaíocht na Comhairle Oidhreachta ar feadh na mblianta ríthábhachtach agus leanúnach. Ba mhaith liom buíochas a ghlacadh le Bord agus le Foireann na Comhairle Oidhreachta as a dtiomantas i leith na hoidhreachta ar fud na hÉireann.

Ceann de na príomhthorthaí a bhí ar an gcéad suirbhé ar thuí i Laoise ná gur theastaigh níos mó tacaíochta ó úinéirí tithe ceann tuí ó thaobh eolas praiticiúil a bheith ar fáil chun tacú leo a dtithe a chaomhnú agus chomh tábhachtach céanna, maoiniú a bheith ar fáil chun an obair leanúnach a bhíonn riachtanach chun na tithe seo a choinneáil ar an bhfód a dhéanamh.

Ghlac Comhairle Chontae Laoise céim thábhachtach chun go leor de na tithe seo a chur ar Thaifead na Struchtúr Cosanta rud a thabharfaidh cosaint dlí láidir do na tithe seo agus cuirfidh sé ar chumas úinéirí maoiniú a fháil d'obair chaomhnaithe ní hamháin i leith na tuí ach i leith gnéithe eile de na tithe seo chomh maith a chuireann lena luach stairiúil- fuinneoga, dorais agus gnéithe bunaidh eile ina measc. Molaim do na húineirí ar fad a bhfuil a gcuid tithe ar Thaifead na Struchtúr Cosanta an maoiniú seo a fháil.

Tá súil agam go mbainfidh úinéirí na dtithe ceann tuí ar fad, na daoine a bhfuil cuimhní cinn acu ar thithe ceann tuí agus aon duine eile a bhfuil suim acu in oidhreacht Chontae Laoise sult as an leabhar seo.

Peter Carey
Bainisteoir Contae

We are the voices of these houses.

*The houses cannot speak for themselves,
so we have to speak for them.*

If we don't speak, they won't survive.

—Kay Moore

COUNTING HOUSES

On 27 April 1911, a man named Edward M. Hogan passed through the townland of Raheenahoran on the Heath, about four miles from Maryborough. As an enumerator for the 1911 Census, part of Mr Hogan's job was to help document the county's housing stock for the British Government. He counted eight houses in Raheenahoran that day. The largest was a fine five-room farmhouse. The smallest house had just one windowless room, inhabited by an elderly bachelor.

Among the houses Hogan recorded was a two-room stone-walled dwelling inhabited by James and Ellen Bates and their six children, who ranged in age from 15 to two. Its outbuildings included a henhouse and a piggery.

All the houses in Raheenahoran were thatched, as Hogan noted in the Roofs column of the Building Return for the townland. There was nothing unusual about that. In 1911, slightly more than half of the county's houses had thatched roofs.

The idea that a thatched house would ever be remarkable would have been bizarre to Edward Hogan. As strange as if you had told him that one day 15-year-old Patrick Bates in House Number Six would be a member of the winning Laois team in the first National Football League final and fullback on the first Leinster team to win the Railway Cup.

On that day in 1911 Paddy Bates was just another son of an agricultural labourer in a county of farmers, publicans and small shopkeepers. His house was just an ordinary, homemade, everyday thatched house.

The 1911 Census found a total of 11,523 private dwellings in Queen's County, of which 5,779 (50.2%) had thatched roofs and 5,744 (49.8%) had roofs of slate. Fewer than ten percent had walls of mud rather than stone or brick. Only ten percent of legal public houses were thatched.

One hundred years after the 1911 Census, fewer than 40 thatched houses are inhabited on a regular basis. Three thatched pubs continue to trade.

A century after the 1911 Census, a thatched house in Laois is as rare as the corncrake. In 1911, more than half of the county's houses were thatched; today only 34 of these historic thatched roofs remain, although, in some places, the old thatched roofs still survive under sheets of corrugated iron.

Some families have cherished and maintained their thatched houses for generations. Others associate the old thatched houses with harder times and a way of life that, mercifully, has passed.

Today, the challenge is to conserve the best aspects of the old thatched houses—such as their thick walls and insulating, locally sourced roofs—while helping them become vital, functioning houses for 21st century families.

Like any task worth doing, it is not easy. And in difficult economic times, the fate of the thatched houses of Laois appears even more uncertain. But one thing is clear: once the historic thatched houses go, an important part of what makes Laois itself will also be gone.

If you scratch the ancestors of any of our people you'll discover that they all came from mud-walled thatched houses. Centuries ago, when most of them were tenant farmers and labourers and they had almost nothing, they were able to take indigenous materials — just mud, straw, wood and stone — and built a warm and comfortable place to live.

That's the primary reason these houses have to be preserved today, when so many people have lost all connection with where they came from, particularly during the Celtic Tiger years. We have to rediscover where we came from if we're going to rise from the ashes now.

— Jackie Hyland

Thatch in Laois today

A survey of the thatched houses of Laois, conducted in 2007 and updated in 2010, recorded a total of 61 sites of thatched buildings, including farmhouses, urban dwellings, public houses and ruins. In 34 of these thatched buildings, the early roof structures and historic thatch (original and early layers of straw roofing) remained intact and the building was still usable as a home or a pub premises.

The greatest number of thatched structures was found in the north and north-east of the county. Twenty-six thatched structures were located in or near Mountmellick, Ballyfin, Emo, Ballybrittas, Fisherstown and Vicarstown. Eleven more were found near Cullahill, Abbeyleix, Ballacolla and Clough. Isolated thatched houses were found near Stradbally, Ballylynan, Rosenallis, Clonaslee, Rushin, Errill, Rathdowney and Ullard.

Thatched buildings seemed to have completely disappeared from the south-east and south-west of the county. None remained in the Borris-in-Ossory area or near the Carlow border, although thatch may survive under galvanised roofs in those areas.

As well as historic thatched buildings, which were standing long before the 1911 Census, the county also contains several new and replica thatched structures. Among them is The Poet's Cottage near Camross, which operates as a heritage centre.

I love the look of a newly thatched house...the lovely golden colour of it and the way the scollops are done at the top, you know, criss-cross and all that. It looks lovely with the white wall.

—Mary Bergin

The Poet's Cottage

Opposite page: Laois Thatcher Jimmy Dowling at work

STRUCTURE

Every thatched house in Laois was built of locally sourced materials. Using fieldstone and other rocks, people constructed walls that they plastered into place with mud. In places where stone was scarce, they mixed mud with grasses and twigs and other materials, then, using farm animals or their own feet, trampled this mixture until it took shape as firm clay. Using a piece of yarn or twine, they cut the clay into blocks, which were stacked like bricks. The final step would have been to smooth the sides into a wall using the flat side of a tool and their hands.

The one-room depth of most of these houses is probably due in some part to the length of timbers available to create an A-frame roof. Wood was sourced from local trees. If trees were scarce, people went to the bogs for bog oak and other wood from ancient forests.

They constructed a roof by resting the long timbers directly on top of the house's walls. The long timbers that formed the A shape of the roof were braced by horizontal collar timbers (each one was positioned between a pair of long timbers like the stroke in the middle of the letter A). Wooden pegs or nails held the long timbers and bracing collar timbers in place.

On top of the timbers went a layer of scraw: carpet-like lengths of turf or sod laid to form the first layer of a tight roof. Rather than meeting at the top, which would have made a seam that could have let in water, these pieces lapped over it, and slightly over each other, forming a weather-tight ridge.

Some years ago, the thatching of a house was a matter of great importance. The professional thatcher was provided with special fare and he got a glass of whiskey each morning before starting on the day's work.... The best thatcher was the man who knew how to put the proper slope on the house at the top of the house so that no water would sink into the roof.

— Áine Bean Uí Ciarbaic of Stradbally, recorded by the Irish Folklore Commission in 1945

Lengths of scraw, laid like pieces of carpet, cover the rafters of this house. They were used to anchor the thatch.

To make scraw, you'd go up to the mountain bog where there would be grass and heather. You'd cut your scraw maybe two foot wide and maybe ten foot long, then roll it up. You'd let it dry in the summertime. When the weight had gone out of it, you'd bring it home and put it up on the new roof, then roll it down like a carpet. It would be stitched on then. It would be about four or five inches in thickness. Once that was done, you'd have a grip for the scollop in the scraw.

— SEAMUS CONROY

In some areas, like Ballybrittas, this first layer of roofing was made from the branches of local pine trees: needles, pinecones and all. Whether it was made from scraw or branches, the first layer was tied to the timbers with grass súgán rope or, in later years, twine. Once the base layer was in place, the roof was ready to be thatched.

In the damp Irish climate, these houses have been baked into existence from the inside out. Fires on the internal open hearth, and in later years, in various types of stoves and ranges, have driven the damp from the stone and mud walls and helped dry the thatch and slow its rotting.

In bygone times, the daily fire—which kept the family warm, cooked the food and boiled the water for washing—also kept the house in good condition. Even today, unless these houses are regularly "aired" by heat or an internal fire, they will rapidly begin to deteriorate.

The side ends of thatched houses have two basic forms. In gable-ended houses, the end walls of the house extend all the way up to the ridge of the roof. In hipped roofs, like this one on a small house in Rosenallis, the roof extends down to the end wall, as it does to the walls at the front and back. Both hipped and gable-ended roofs are found in County Laois, although gable-ended roofs are more common.

THATCHING

Historically there have been two common ways of thatching a house in Laois: scollop thatching and thrust thatching. With scollop thatching, oaten or wheaten straw is secured to the base layer with scollops: pieces of hazel, willow, bramble or other flexible wood.

A straight, horizontal scollop holds bundles of straw in place on the surface of the roof. Then a hairpin scollop—which is twisted in half—is hammered in, so that it pins the bundle of straw to the layers below. It springs back, "stapling" the thatch in place. It is important that the scollops are hammered well into the thatch; any left exposed could catch rainwater, which would lead to the thatch rotting.

While scollop thatching is the most common method used in Laois today, some thatchers prefer thrust thatching. In this method, the thatcher uses a thatching fork to force a tied bundle of straw into the existing thatch, building up layer upon layer.

The final stage of thatching is like a gigantic haircut. The thatcher walks around the edges of the house, trimming the fresh hanging thatch with a pair of shears. The thick overhang ensures that rain does not come in contact with the walls, but runs off onto the ground.

Ridges

The steeply pitched roof characteristic of thatched houses ensures that rainwater runs off the roof quickly. To maintain the steep roof, thatchers must build up the ridge whenever the house is re-thatched.

While ridge types vary, the main type used in Laois is the comb ridge, also known as a twisted bobbin ridge. To make this ridge, a bundle of straw is twisted at the centre to produce a knot, or bobbin.

Several bobbins are then threaded onto a scollop, or stick, to form a section of ridge comb. The ridge comb is placed over the roof's ridge like a saddle, then secured in place by one or more rows of horizontal scollops.

Decorative end knobs are sometimes placed to each end of the ridge. Different thatchers use different styles of knots and ridge finishes; sometimes people can tell who thatched the house by the style of the ridge.

While the twisted bobbin ridge is the most common style used in the county, less elaborate ridge types are also found. One is the lap-over ridge, which is made by placing a bundle of thatch over the ridge and securing it to the front and back slopes with scollops. Another type is the butt-up ridge, in which the end pieces of the bundles of thatch meet at the apex of the roof.

Sometimes, elaborate block ridges are found on roofs that have been re-thatched with water reed. However, this ridge type, like the use of water reed itself, is not traditional in Laois.

A really warm day would be ideal. When you'd splash the whitewash onto the house, you'd nearly hear it sizzle. That would be a real good day. It would stick really well. Sometimes you'd have to wash the splashes off the window. . . .

Everybody [all six children] would want to do it at first, but then it would be left to whoever would mainly be doing it. The second storey, that would be for my father to do.

—Kay Moore

Whitewash

Traditionally the thatched houses of Laois are whitewashed each year with a mixture of lime and water. Sometimes natural pigments or ochres are added to the mixture to give a subtle colour to the finished house, but usually the mixture is left in its natural white state.

Unlike a nonporous render, the whitewash lets moisture pass out through the house walls. Over time, layers of whitewash build up, giving a velvet-like finish to the houses.

Bluestone

Most owners of thatched houses spray their roofs each year with a solution of water and copper sulphate, also called bluestone. This helps maintain the colour of the straw and slows its deterioration, probably by discouraging fungal growth. Copper sulphate's anti-fungal properties are also why it has been sprayed on potatoes since 1882 to prevent blight.

Doors

In the earliest thatched houses open doors were the main source of light. They also let out smoke.

Even after windows became common, glass was a luxury item and windows tended to be small. During daylight hours, the open door was the major source of light for a thatched house. Half doors let in fresh air and light while keeping animals out. They also kept small children inside.

The well-maintained whitewashed wall of a pub provided the perfect backdrop for this picture from 1972, courtesy of Kenneth Keogh.

Bluestone solution running off the thatch has stained a white-washed wall at Abbeyview Cottage, the family home of Michael Dempsey.

Although the closed bottom of a traditional half door is supposed to keep out animals, that is not always the case. The Dunne brothers' Jack Russell was famous for its ability to leap in and out of the front door of their house near Clonaghadoo (yellow door above).

For the peahen on Bridie Lewis's farm, the half door of a farmyard building is merely another perch from which she can survey her demesne.

Hens hatching chicks during the winter were once brought inside to stay in this hen house, which sits in the kitchen of Bridie Lewis's farmhouse. Today it is used for storage.

The hearth was so wide that you sat in on a form — a board seat attached to the wall — under the chimney when you were by the fire. Inside the chimney, the walls were black from all the fires that had been burned there.

If you looked up, you could see the sky and clouds above, and chicken wire across the top to keep the birds out. It was a huge opening. A person could get up inside the chimney if they wanted to, and gradually it got smaller toward the top.

Sometimes, a few raindrops would come down. You'd hear a hiss when they hit the hearth.

— Clare Mulhall

Facing page: the canopy over the hearth, a rare feature in Laois, was usually made of woven sticks plastered with mud. Sometimes partition walls inside thatched houses, which were often made after the house had been roofed, were also made of this material.

Form

The thatched houses of Laois have two basic floor plans, the direct-entry house plan and the lobby-entry house plan.

In direct-entry thatched houses, the main door opens directly into the kitchen. At one end of the kitchen, the hearth is located on an internal wall. Side rooms are accessed directly off the central kitchen.

In lobby-entry thatched houses, the front door opens onto a small lobby, which is created by a jamb wall. Because it is perpendicular to the hearth, the jamb wall acts as a windbreak. Some jamb walls contain a small "spy window" that allows a person seated at the hearth to see anyone entering the house. As with direct-entry houses, the central kitchen provides access to rooms on either side of the house.

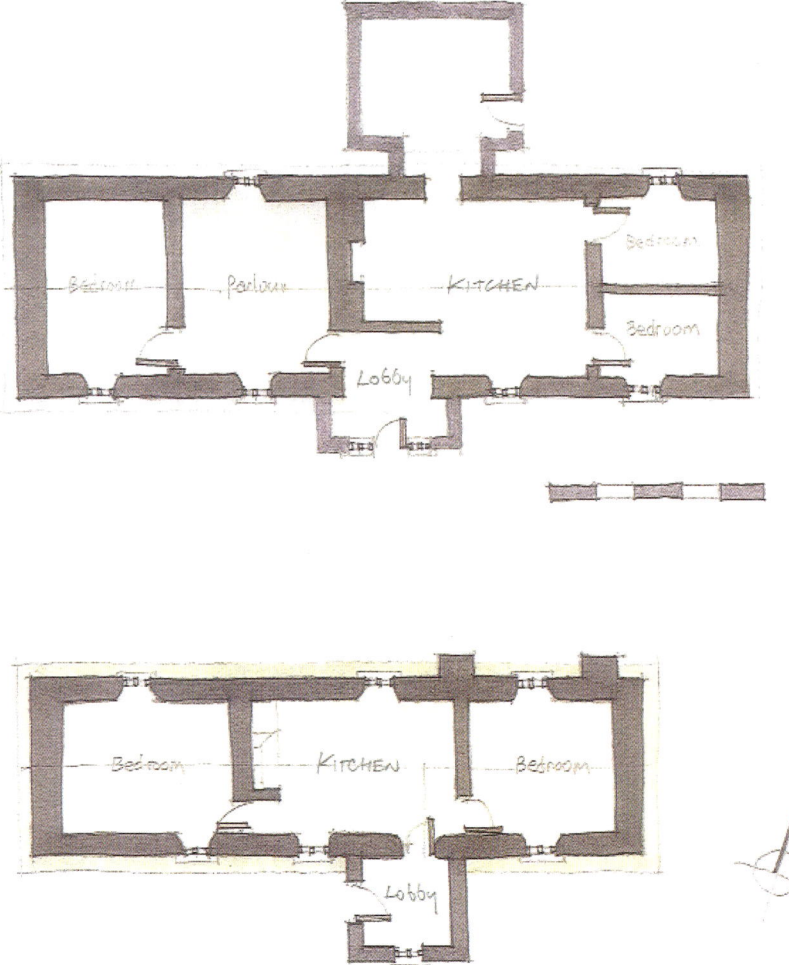

Houseleek

Growing out of the side of this Laois farmhouse is a succulent plant called Houseleek (*Sempervivum tectorum*). For centuries, people throughout Europe have planted houseleeks on their roofs and walls to ward off lightning, fire and evil spirits. The earliest recorded instance of this practice dates to 4 BC.

This five-bay thatched house near Mountmellick belongs to Liam and Abigail McEvoy. It was thatched by the late Sean Brennan, who was extremely well-regarded by many thatched house owners before he passed away. Most recently it was thatched by another respected thatcher in the county, Seamus Conroy.

A House of History: Abbeyview Cottage

Because the design, layout, building styles and materials of thatched houses changed so little over the centuries, it can be very difficult to know when a house was built or how it changed over time. An exception to this rule is Abbeyview Cottage, near Fisherstown. Thanks to the keen interest of Michael Dempsey, who combines the knowledge of a skilled craftsman with the curiosity of a detective, we know more about Abbeyview Cottage than about any other thatched house in Laois.

The house has belonged to the Dempsey family since the early 1900s.

As Michael has renovated and cared for Abbeyview Cottage over the years, he has made discoveries that extend back to the building of the house. While working beneath the roof, he found that the rafters were made of Scots Pine from local trees. "No part of the tree was wasted, the trunk was split, the lower ends were bedded in the mud wall, and the upper ends of the rafters were chiselled out to connect with the opposite rafter by way of an oak peg hammered through," he says. "The lighter parts of the tree were used to make runners and collar ties. These also were held together with oak dowels."

Rather than turf scraw, the layer on the rafters that anchored the thatch was made out of the tips of pine branches. Some still had pinecones attached. Michael sent a number of these pinecones off to the Radiocarbon Laboratory at University College Dublin. According to Dr Edward McGee, one pinecone probably grew on a tree in Laois between 1414 and 1642, with the most likely date being 1468.

When I was going to school, there were 32 thatched houses around here. Only four of those are still standing, and now there are about 32 thatched houses left in the whole county.

—Michael Dempsey

On top of the pine branches, the first layer of thatch was made of wheaten straw. There were also layers of thatch made from the straw of barley and oats. Most of the scollops used to hold the thatch in place on the roof were pieces of two-year-old hazel, although the roof also contains twigs of oak, sally, ash and elm, which were probably harvested from local hedges.

At one place in the roof, the straw was blackened with soot, a sign that before the house had a chimney, smoke from the hearth passed straight up through the thatched roof.

Although it was built without a formal plan, Abbeyview Cottage demonstrates the excellent craftsmanship of the people who built it. "The work of the stonemasons on the extension to the original house is incredible; we think it must have been added on around 1800. And the timber in the doors and windows is still perfect. They look as if they could last another century," Michael says.

When he was growing up, the family story was that a priest had lived in the house. By examining local records, Michael has determined that the priest was Reverend Daniel Maher, who is listed in the Catholic Directory of 1835. He also believes that a hatch between the parlour and the kitchen of Abbeyview Cottage was probably used by a housekeeper to pass food through to the priest at mealtime.

Michael Dempsey

Michael Dempsey places a hairpin scollop into position, before hammering it in to hold the straight scollop that will secure a fresh layer of thatch.

This mallet will be used to rethatch the worn out roof shown here. The straw has become discoloured with age and the hairpin scollops are sticking up. The straight scollops in this section of the roof have been removed, prior to thatching.

Describing himself as a "hobby thatcher", Michael Dempsey belongs to the long tradition of farmers who grow their own straw and do their own thatching.

Along with his brother, three sisters, parents and grandmother, Michael lived for the first 30 years of his life in a thatched house known as Abbeyview Cottage, not far from Fisherstown. His fascination with thatching began at age six, when his father left behind pits of potatoes, covered with clay and straw, in the farmyard. By the time he had returned from milking that evening, he found that Michael had thatched the pits, and even put a row of bobbins along their tops. "My dad found that very amusing," Michael says.

As a child, Michael helped his father whenever thatching took place. The first time he thatched the roof by himself it lasted for 15 years, far beyond the normal range of 7 to 10 years.

Michael moved out of Abbeyview Cottage in 1967 when he built a bungalow for his new bride, Brigid. Today, his son Oliver operates Abbeyview Cottage as a self-catering holiday home. However, Michael continues to thatch the house on a regular basis, most recently in 1994 and in 2010.

In 2010, Michael's sons Oliver and Martin helped with the thatching. "I wanted to teach Oliver and Martin how to do it, in case I'm not around the next time it needs to be done," Michael says.

While a paid thatcher could complete a roof in about 12 days, Michael and his sons can take a few weeks to rethatch the house, fitting in the thatching work around milking and other jobs on the farm. Being able to take his time with the job allows Michael to be a perfectionist.

As well as making the line of twisted bobbins that go along the ridge of the roof, Michael makes a knob of straw, topped by a round copper plate, for each corner.

"It's lovely to shape the straw…and there's a certain satisfaction in seeing the finished product," he says.

Martin and Michael Dempsey twist blades of grass together to make súgán, the type of rope that has been used for centuries to tie the base layer of turf or branches to the rafters of a thatched roof. Two lengths of this rope twisted together are strong enough to pull a cart. In the past it was also used to fashion furniture and baskets.

HARVEST

When a house needs thatching, farmers traditionally have grown the oats themselves.

Neighbours help Bridie Lewis and Ned Ging harvest oats to thatch their house. Matt Hyland drives that tractor, while Louis Troy operates the reaper and binder that cuts and binds the sheaves of oats.

After it is cut, a band of friends and neighbours helps stack the sheaves into "stooks".

Once the oats have matured, they are put through an old threshing mill, which separates out the grain while keeping the straw long enough to be used for thatch. The oats are then used for feed.

Practical skills

For centuries, a thatched roof was the most practical option, particularly for farmers who could grow and cut their own straw. Thatching skills were passed from father to son and neighbour to neighbour.

As people became more prosperous and work became more specialised, thatching became a profession in its own right. Seamus Conroy was taught by a full-time thatcher named Ted McEvoy. Around 1964 or 1965 McEvoy would have charged 8 or 9 Irish pounds for a week of thatching. Most of his materials would have been grown by local farmers. Today, Conroy says, labour costs more than materials.

Scollops

It takes hundreds of scollops—sharpened pieces of flexible wood, such as hazel or willow—to thatch or rethatch a roof. For centuries, Laois men and women have used sharp tools, such as billhooks, to cut scollops from hedges and scrubland. Once they have been harvested, each end of a scollop is pointed with three cuts: one long cut, then two short cuts on the sides. About 4,000 scollops are necessary for an average roof.

There used to be a good few thatchers. There would be nine or ten in a parish, and then there would also be men who would do their own houses.

— Seamus Conroy

At the Fisherman's Inn, a thatched pub in Fisherstown, the outer layers of thatch are of oaten straw, but the earlier layers, including the soot-saturated base coat, are made of wheaten straw. This is also true for many of the county's houses.

WHEAT, OATS AND REED

To thatch their houses, people have used whatever straw came from local cereal crops, whether it was wheat, oats or barley. Wheaten straw was widely used in Laois until the middle of the 20th century, when farmers began to spray their crops with chemicals to regulate growth, which resulted in shorter shafts that were unsuitable for thatch.

Today the most commonly used thatching material in Laois is oaten straw, although some houses are thatched with water reed. Oaten straw is prized for its beautiful golden colour. Depending on a number of factors—the quality of the straw, the skill of the thatcher, the siting of the house and the weather—a roof thatched with oaten straw can last from 7 to 15 years. Water reed, which comes from other parts of Ireland or may be imported from Turkey or Poland, is reputed to last longer than oaten straw, but has a different effect and is not traditional to County Laois.

HOMEPLACE

The Dowling family around 1950. Back row: Tom, Nora, Mike, Bertie, Margaret. Middle Row: Mary, Lee, Anne. Front row: Pat, Jimmy on John Dowling's knee, Eileen, Phil, Bridie, Kathleen on Ellen Dowling's knee and John. Teresa, the youngest, does not appear in this photo.

When Ellen Doran married John Dowling and came to live in his thatched house near Emo, she was 19 years old. She lived there until she passed away at age 97. Over the decades, the Dowlings' house became virtually a family member in its own right. Whenever Ellen and John Dowling were photographed with their 16 children, they all lined up in front of the house.

When Theresa Delahunty "married into" her thatched house near Durrow, it had been in her husband's family for three generations. At that time, the house had a settlebed and a dresser in its kitchen, which was open to the rafters above. Since then, the house has seen some changes, including the addition of tongue-and-groove ceilings to the kitchen, lobby and parlour, and a hot press extension opposite the kitchen wall. The house was last thatched with oaten straw by Jackie Kavanagh in 2000.

Some thatched houses have been home to the same family for seven or eight generations. When a group of thatched house owners met in Abbeyleix in May 2010, three of the women present still cared for the thatched houses in which they had been born. Two of them had never lived anywhere else.

In the past, it was common for larger families to live in smaller houses than they do today. As well as sleeping in designated bedrooms, family members might sleep in fold-down press beds in the parlour or in a settlebed near the kitchen fire.

When the need arose for more space, the houses, which were usually one room deep and one storey high, were often extended from the ends.

Nancy Phelan's House

Nancy Phelan lives in a thatched house in the shadow of Cullahill Castle. The house came into her family when her grandparents bought it from Mrs Honoria Kenney, who had a small greengrocer's shop there. Mrs Phelan was born in her house and has lived there her entire life.

When she was growing up, Nancy Phelan's father told her that a room had been added on to one end of the house sometime during its history. Then, around 1940, the house was extended because her father's aunt needed a place to live. Her father built two extra bedrooms onto the back of the house, on the other side of the kitchen wall. Mrs Phelan can recall seeing the original mud wall of the kitchen being propped up while her father cut the two new doors that led into these bedrooms.

Mrs Phelan's house was thatched with oaten straw until she found that it was difficult to obtain. Recently Mrs Phelan had the house thatched with reed, with the hope that the roof will not have to be thatched again during her lifetime.

Left: Nancy Phelan in front of her house

Four or five of us used to sleep in the settle bed when we were little lads. It was in the kitchen close to the fire, and in the daytime it was folded up against the wall with a few cushions behind it for a seat.

At night-time you'd be in bed half-asleep and when my father would come in from the pub, you'd hear him talking, you know. It was lovely….

—Jimmy Dowling

Jimmy Dowling

Jimmy Dowling was one of 16 children that grew up in a small thatched house near Emo. The house had been purchased by his grandfather when he returned to the area after living in America.

Jimmy can't remember living in the house before it had electricity, but he has vivid memories of bringing in water from the pump and bathing in a big steel tub on the floor. When asked what it was like to live in his house as a child, he says: "Very busy you'd be. You'd be working the time. Sure the mother of us all must have been made of steel…."

The house was so much a part of the family that the children always gathered to have their pictures taken in front of it, including the last picture taken just months before their mother, Ellen Dowling, died.

Jimmy has found that his interest in thatching as grown in recent years. Three years ago he took the thatching course in Portumna, then got some on-the-job training with Seamus Conroy. He now finds farming and thatching a good combination.

Since the death of his mother, he has renovated his family's thatched house with a view to letting it to holiday makers.

Throughout Laois, photo albums contain pictures of thatched family homes, many of which no longer exist. Top: family home on the Heath, courtesy of Maria Hyland. Centre left: Bergin family home at Ballytarsna, Pike of Rushall, courtesy of Tony Bergin. Centre right: Keogh family home in Huntington, Portarlington, courtesy of Kenneth Keogh. Bottom: Lesley Bailey's house near Portarlington, courtesy of Lesley Bailey.

A Happy Family Home: The House at Jamestown Cross

What do I remember about growing up in that house? Well, number one: I loved it. We had a wonderful home life and we had wonderful parents.

Number two: My sisters were very fond of dancing. And every fortnight or three weeks or so we'd be allowed to have a dance in the kitchen. It had a floor of washed cement and sand. It was as smooth as that wall.

Our cousins were all musicians and they taught us how to dance. All around the kitchen and mind the dresser was the only thing.

—Margaret McLoughlin Mulhall

If ever there was a happy family home it was located in the thatched house at Jamestown Cross, where Margaret "Madge" McLoughlin Mulhall grew up with her sisters Lil and Lena and her brothers Tom and Jimmy. The house came into the family during the nineteenth century, after her great-grandmother, a widow with three small children, was evicted from a house at the Windmill near Killenard.

The McLoughlin family lived an almost entirely self-sufficient life. They grew all their vegetables, made jam and tarts with fruit from their trees, and baked their bread in a cast iron baker over the fire. On Fridays, they churned their milk to make butter and buttermilk. Every October they killed a pig and hung the cured meat on hooks in the kitchen, to be used throughout the rest of the year.

The McLoughlins grew the oats they used to thatch their house, and harvested scollops from the hedges nearby. They hired a local thatcher, rather than doing the thatching themselves.

Possibly the best time of the year was threshing season. For about six weeks groups of men moved from one farm to another threshing wheat, barley and oats. At night they would return home to clean up and shave. Then around nine they'd meet in the kitchen of one of the farms for music,

Thatched houses are very warm. The frost comes on the roof, but it doesn't have any effect. And they're cooler in the summer. At one point they thought about putting slates or galvanised sheeting on the roof, but my brother Tom wouldn't change. He said: 'If it's good enough for my grandfather, it's good enough for me.'

— MARGARET MULHALL

For years tour buses passing along the old main road from Dublin to Cork would halt at Jamestown Cross so that their occupants could be photographed standing in front of the McLoughlins' thatched house. Tom McLoughlin and his sister Lil often offered the tourists mugs of "leaf tea": real tea, not the kind made with tea bags. It was not unusual, weeks later, for the McLoughlins to receive a letter from a far off place that contained a picture of Tom and Lil standing in front of their house.

dancing and "junction cake". Mrs Mulhall can remember being whirled around the kitchen at Jamestown Cross by one of her cousins, while his brothers played the tin whistle and the concertina.

After school, the McLoughlin children played in the field across from their house. One brother, Tom, was so skilled at skittles he was known as "Spring" for the rest of his days. When Mrs Mulhall was eight years old, a man from Kilkenny and another from Tipperary, who were building the church over at St Anne's, began to train local children in hurling and camogie on Sunday afternoons. The three McLoughlin sisters played on the Jamestown Camogie Club team and the Laois team into their thirties. Lil, in particular, won many medals because "she was quicker than the ball".

The McLoughlin family studied and spoke Irish at home. Their house was used as a station house, where the local priest collected dues at Christmas and Easter.

Throughout her childhood, there is only one thing Mrs Mulhall did not like about her house: the sound of the old grandfather clock on the wall. "We hated when it used to strike. Unfortunately every hour."

Except for a brief period when she worked in Dublin, Mrs Mulhall lived in the house and worked on the farm until she married Pat Mulhall, a man from the parish whom she describes as "the best husband any woman ever had". The last family member to live in the house was her sister Lil Coleman, who passed away in October 2009.

The Rarest of Them All: Crannagh House

Crannagh House is a rarity: one of the last surviving two-storey thatched farmhouses in Ireland. For decades it was the home of Joan and Dan Dunne, who raised their six children on the family farm there.

Kay Dunne Moore, the last child born in the house, remembers the work of caring and maintaining the house as part of the rhythm of life on the farm. Before Crannagh House got running water, the children took turns bringing water in from the pump in the garden. "We used to go to the pump for water to fill up the tank beside the cooker in the kitchen," Kay explains. "Or we'd go down to the pump to wash the potatoes or to get a drink sometimes or just to splash in the water on a hot day."

During summers, the children vied with each other to help their father whitewash the house. Dan Dunne also thatched the house himself, growing oats in his own fields.

Every room of Crannagh House and every field of its farm had a special name and purpose: the Little Parlour was where the men went to eat during threshing season. The four Dunne girls slept, two to a bed, in the Far Room. The boys slept in the Big Room, which was right over the kitchen. The Lower Room was a bedroom on the ground floor, opposite the parlour. "It was all very well laid out for a house of that time," Kay says.

While it was homely, Crannagh House was not particularly warm in the winter. The family and visitors spent most of their time in the kitchen—the warmest room in the house—or they'd light a fire in the parlour.

"When we'd wake up in the morning it would be freezing. And you'd most times get dressed in the kitchen," Kay says. "Mammy would always be sure to have the fire going, to have the cooker lit. There was a rack over the cooker and she'd have the clothes on that so your clothes would be warm.

Summers, on the other hand, were divine. "The house was lovely and cool," Kay says. "It seemed to get a new lease of life."

Although the kitchen was small for such a large house, it was full nearly every night with "ramblers": friends and neighbours who would stop by after supper for a chat, a cup of tea or a game of poker or 25.

When Kay finished school during the 1980s, there was little work to be had. Before she was launched into adult life, she spent the better part of one summer helping her father collect scollops to re-thatch the roof. At night Kay sat with her father by the fire paring scollops and talking.

The deep windows of Crannagh House held ornaments and religious pictures. At night the family closed the shutters to keep in the warmth.

My father, Dan Dunne, used to say that any country can be defined by its buildings. That's what makes thatched houses so important. They're part of our heritage. They've been associated with Ireland going back many years....when you learn about them, they tell you about the lives of the people who lived in them.

— Kay Moore

Crannagh House is one of the last two-storey thatched dwellings left in Ireland.

After all the children had grown up and left home, Crannagh House entered a period of crisis. Once Dan Dunne was no longer able to thatch the roof, it began to decay. But for the skill and expertise of Seamus Conroy from Clonaslee, Kay is certain the house would have been lost.

Mr Conroy sourced thatch and nearly 7,000 scollops for Crannagh House. His work was nothing less than heroic, according to the Dunnes and Moores.

"I can't speak highly enough of Seamus," Kay says. "He told my father that from the time he attended national school he loved the thatch and always hoped he could save some of these houses. Seamus gave Crannagh a new lease of life. He saved it from falling."

No family members presently live in Crannagh House, but all of them continue to take a keen interest in maintaining it. From time to time, Mary Dunne lights a fire in the kitchen stove to keep the house aired until it is occupied again.

Seamus Conroy

When he was 17, Seamus Conroy was taught to thatch by his neighbour, Ted McEvoy. The next time his own house needed thatching, Mr Conroy's father let him do the job. It lasted for 11 years, which was impressive since thatching can often last only as long as five or six years. Mr Conroy had found his vocation.

For nearly 50 years Mr Conroy has thatched houses in Laois and Offaly, as well as doing some farming and silage contract work.

"When I began there was a fierce lot more thatched houses than there are now," he says. "Then the roofs were taken off and replaced with slated and galvanised roofs, although I've done a few where we took off the galvanised roofs and replaced the thatch."

Mr Conroy has helped train some of the new thatchers in the county, including Philip Doran and Jimmy Dowling. His own style of thatching is scollop thatching, in which the straw is pinned to the roof with scollops, rather than thrust thatching in which bundles of straw are thrust into the roof with a special fork. "Thrust thatching is okay for doing a roof in good condition, but if it's in any way bad, you're better off scolloping," he explains.

Since Mr Conroy suffered an illness two years ago, his son Ivor has begun to take over the thatching business.

Kay Dunne Moore was the last child to be born in Crannagh House. She poses here with a self-portrait of her grandmother, Emily Lynch Williams, who was also born in Crannagh House and grew up there.

Kay Moore credits thatcher Seamus Conroy with saving Crannagh House, one of the rare surviving two-storey thatched houses in Laois.

A Time Capsule: The House at Clonaghadoo

Anyone walking into the tiny lobby of the thatched house at Clonaghadoo is greeted by a framed photograph of the actress June Haver. With her tight sweater, red lipstick and machine perm, she looks both wholesome and luscious, a scrumptious version of a *bean an tí*.

No woman has resided in the Dunne family's thatched house since 1948, when Elizabeth Dunne passed away, after rearing seven sons and one grandson with her husband William. Today the house is owned and maintained by Elizabeth and William's great-grandson, Eddie Dunne, who keeps it just as it was when his uncles and great uncles lived there.

In the small lobby of the house there's a tall narrow cavity in the wall. Today it contains light switches, but during the War of Independence, this hollow was plastered over so that the wall looked unbroken. Rifles used by the local branch of the Irish Republican Army were stashed inside.

During his youth the house was "men only" according to Eddie Dunne. On any given night 12 to 14 men would crowd into the kitchen, talking, telling stories and playing cards. The open hearth worked, if anything, too well. It was not unusual to hear a man, who had had his turn close to the fire, stand up and announce: "I'm half cooked".

The Dunne brothers finally got electricity in the 1970s, but otherwise, they lived in the house pretty much as they always had. They took their water from the pump just outside the door, and cooked over the open hearth. A fork that hung on the wall was used to turn bacon or rashers in a huge cast iron pan. Two of the uncles slept together in a settle bed, which was folded down in the kitchen each night.

The last of the uncles, Billy Dunne, was tragically killed as he cycled home in 1994. Since that time, Eddie has kept the house in good repair. "I'll keep it as long as I'm here," he says.

Eddie Dunne and his son Edward stand in the doorway of the house at Clonaghadoo. When the Dunne brothers lived here, the door was left open summer and winter because of the heat of the fire and the good insulation. The brothers' dog was famous for its ability to jump in and out of the half door.

William and Elizabeth Dunne raised their seven sons and one grandson, in the three-roomed house at Clonaghadoo. Since Billy Dunne passed away in 1994, the house has been maintained by his nephew, Eddie Dunne, who has a farm nearby.

During the Troubles, the boys were all involved in the IRA, which was the standing army at the time. And the Black and Tans were always searching the house and threatening to burn it down. My uncles used to keep the sticks of gelignite along the bottom of that dresser, where you couldn't see them. One time my grandmother heard the Black and Tans pull up outside to search the house. That was back when women used to wear long bibs, and they used to carry things in them. So my grandmother gathered up all the gelignite from the dresser and put it in the fold of her bib. Then she walked out into the yard, making a noise like she was about to feed the hens, and walked on toward the Central Lane. The Black and Tans had been tipped off about the gelignite, but they didn't pay any attention to the old woman who was going past them as they came into the house.

— EDDIE DUNNE

The open hearth was the scene of many debates. Among the topics were: 1) the number of pheasants someone had shot, 2) the way the country was going and 3) land reclamation. Most of the county's drains have been drawn—both the way they went and the way they should have gone—in the ash pit near the hearth.

This pump, attached to the well outside the house at Clonaghadoo, supplied the Dunne family with water.

Like most families, the Dunnes displayed their best delft on the dresser in the kitchen.

ALL MOD CONS

Electricity was the first thing that came in the 1950s. We got it early, probably because of our proximity to Portlaoise, but I remember that it was about seven years later that it came to my maternal grandparents' place. Until it arrived they were using the Tilley lamps, in which you pumped up the fuel into the wick. They gave quite a good light, certainly better than candle light.

—Jackie Hyland

While many of the county's thatched houses may have been pleasant to live in throughout their long history, others were damp, low and dark. During the twentieth century, new stoves, electricity and running water made many thatched houses more comfortable.

Until 1959, when the Dempsey family installed a Stanley cooker, the draft of the open fire sucked all the heat out of the house, according to Michael Dempsey. "Before the stove there was really only one place that was warm, and that was the seat right next to the fire. There was always a fight to get that seat. And there were big gaps underneath the doors, which didn't help keep the warmth in."

Not everyone embraced these home improvements. At Clonaghadoo, the Dunne brothers refused the Government's offer of electricity the first time it came around in 1960s. Finally, in the 1970s they relented and electric lights replaced the Tilley lamps that had lit the house for years. Still the house never had running water. Its last full-time occupant, Billy Dunne, pumped water from the well just outside the front door and cooked over an open hearth until his death in 1994.

In the late 1960s and 1970s, local councils gave grants so that people could add on more modern toilet and kitchen facilities to their houses. Many owners took advantage of this program and built extensions onto their thatched houses, often in a t-shape to the back of the original house. For example, the McLoughlins at Jamestown Cross converted an outside dairy into a toilet and shower room.

Before we got in the electricity in the early 1950s, our cottage was wired by two local men, Johnny and Andy Whelan. The cost of each light was 10 shillings, the plug socket cost 30 shillings and they also put in a trip switch.

We kept trying out the switches every day to see if the electricity had arrived. When the big day came, the house never looked so bright in its life. We could see into corners and cracks which you would never notice with the old candles or oil lamps.

The wireless and the electric iron—which replaced solid iron and the old box iron— were the first things we got. The wireless was a Philips Electric and cost £19.

Then my father spent a week snagging turnips for delivery by Jimmy Early's lorry to the Dublin market.… On the way home he bought a two bar electric fire for 2 pounds 10 shillings to heat my mother's bedroom, where she was convalescing after an operation.

Later on then we got an electric water pump.…The next thing was a washing machine, a Novum with a mangle to wring out the clothes, which was a great improvement over the old bath and washboard.

—Michael Dempsey

Electricity? Them old wires. Nothing but chewing gum for the rats.
—Har Dunne on why the Dunne brothers refused to have electricity installed in the 1960s

45

A House of Changes: Mary Bergin's House

The house in which Mary Bergin (née Loughman) lives has been in her family "as far as we know back". A lot has changed since she was a little girl who gathered kipeens (small sticks) to stoke the fire on the open hearth.

When Mrs Bergin was a child, her grandmother did baking for the family using traditional cast-iron pots. As a teenager, she saw her mother make clothes with a hand-cranked sewing machine by the light of an oil lamp.

During the 1950s, the house was electrified and the family replaced the open hearth with a series of ovens. Still the family took buckets to the open well for water or used water from the rain barrel that was always in the yard. It wasn't until after Mrs Bergin married her husband, who "married into the house", that the house got running water.

When Mrs Bergin was growing up, the house had two bedrooms, a kitchen and a parlour. She and her husband added on another bedroom and a full bathroom, which was a big help when they had eight children.

Today Mrs Bergin's house has all the advantages of a traditional dwelling: two-foot thick stone walls that hush the outside noise and a two-foot layer of thatch that keeps the house snug in the winter and cool in the summer. But it also has all the modern conveniences.

Mrs Bergin's granddaughters run in and out of "Granny's House" from their parents' bungalow just a few yards away.

"What do you think of your granny's house?" a visitor asked one of them on a summer's day.

She looked up from her colouring, gave a dazzling smile, then ran off to watch the television with her sister in the parlour.

Our hearth was an ordinary open fire beneath the arch. I remember my grandmother baking in a baker over the fire . . . she just floured inside and put the cake in and she'd have the lid heating. The lid would be put on top then and the bread would bake away there.

Then we got what they used to call a Thomas Phelan range, which was an iron top with an oven at the side. We thought it was marvellous. We had that for years and years and years then . . . I was after getting married, I think it was . . . and we bought this Wellstood cooker and it was fitted into the fireplace. There was a tank beside it where you could put in five or six buckets of water which kept hot all the time.

Oh my God. We felt we were the bees knees.

It had a double oven and you were able to keep the meal hot in the bottom oven and this sort of thing. We thought it was great.

—Mary Bergin

There's something homely about a thatched house. They're so comfortable, to start off with. The thatch is very warm really; you'd never be cold in one. And they're very good in the heat. The last week when we had this sudden heat wave, all you would need to do is go in and sit in the sitting room and you'd feel grand and cool.

–Mary Bergin

Jackie Kavanagh

Jackie Kavanagh lives in a thatched house that has been in his family for approximately 50 years. He began thatching as a boy of 15, when Mike Whelan, an older thatcher, was working on the Kavanagh's family home and needed some help. "He trained me and then I kept on going with other thatchers and learning from other houses that I worked on," he says.

He prefers to board in the thatch, a method that is also called "thrust thatching". "Scollops are inclined to show after seven years unless you put a thick layer of straw over them," he explains.

Presently Mr Kavanagh works by himself. "It's hard to get the younger people to do what you were doing," he explains. Today Jackie Kavanagh thatches two or three houses a year in Laois, Tipperary and Kilkenny, as well as thatching and patching the thatch on his own house. He sources the hazel scollops from Durrow Wood and purchases his oaten straw from a supplier near Cullahill.

BUNGALOW BLISS

The past two years have seen an expansion in house building without precedent in this country's history.... [and] shows no sign of slackening. In this situation two considerations arise: a person wanting to build a house should not be put to too much trouble and expense in planning the particular size and style of the house which best suits him and at the same time monotony in house design must be avoided.... Bungalow Bliss contains no less than 80 different plans each of which is acceptable for the purposes of grants payable by my department.

—James Tulley, TD, Minister for Local Government, September 1975

In the late 1960s, the publication of *Bungalow Bliss* by Jack Fitzsimons revolutionised building in rural Ireland. For centuries, people in Laois had built and maintained houses according to the same simple traditional floorplan. *Bungalow Bliss,* which was an architectural do-it-yourself manual, included a thrilling variety of designs.

Bolstered by grants from the government, people in Laois began to build modern bungalows, often in front of the thatched houses in which their families had lived for centuries. In some cases, older relatives continued to live in the thatched houses. Other people, particularly farmers, converted the traditional thatched houses into storage. On many farms, the old house became "the shed".

Without regular fires to drive out the moisture, many traditional thatched houses began to deteriorate. As their roofs fell in and walls began to buckle, knocking down the old thatched house was considered a matter of safety.

In 1959, my parents built a bungalow right in front of that house, across the yard from it. The house was left there empty and, of course, like most Irish houses in that era, if there was no heat kept in them the roof would eventually cave in. When I came home in '68 it was an awful eyesore.

I heard of a guy with a bulldozer. He had a couple of trucks and we just completely levelled the whole thing, you know. It finished up as landfill. We had to dig a big hole at the end of the pasture and the house went into it.

Now I would like to have done something different. Maybe try to reroof it, but the timber was already gone. I thought I was doing the right thing at the time.

— Tom Lawlor

DEATH OF A HOUSE

As the twentieth century progressed, in many cases the death of a house's inhabitant also meant the end of that house. When the thatched houses of Laois were surveyed in 2007, researchers discovered four thatched houses that had fallen into ruin and were beyond rehabilitation. In all cases, they had been vacated in late twentieth century following the death of an inhabitant or the construction of a new modern dwelling.

The House at Pass of the Plumes

Whenever I hear "Caoch O'Leary" by John Keegan, I've always thought that the piper in that poem walked into a house like my grandparents', where the half door was always closed but the full door was always open.

I used to visit my first cousin and his father and mother there. It was a wonderful house. The floor was flagged and there was a big crane hanging over the open fire with pots hanging from it. The house only had the one big room and a bedroom, so my cousin slept in a settle bed near the fire.

When you walked in the door you'd say: "God bless all here" and the response was: "And bless you kindly, sir".

When I visited I used not to see my cousin's father very much because he was out working, but the mother would be there. She used to dress in long black dresses down to her ankles, and boots. And she always wore a hat, even in the house.

Just an ordinary hat on grey hair and she'd go to mass every morning. She'd walk from there to Ballyroan, which is about four or five miles, every morning and when she'd go shopping, she'd walk to Portlaoise. That would be about seven or eight miles, I suppose. They had no transport of any type. There was nothing like buses or anything in those days. She lived to be a great age, too.

I remember she was of a very happy disposition. They never wanted any more than what they had. Never envied anybody. That was their life and they accepted their life and that was it.

I'm not sure but I think my uncle died first, and then she died. The house was empty after that, kind of abandoned. My father wanted to buy it and keep it as a family home. He went to the bank and managed to get 100 pounds, which was a lot of money in those days, and tried to buy the house, but the landlord wouldn't sell it. Eventually it was bulldozed.

It's only an ordinary field now. It would have been lovely to preserve it.

— Kevin Higgins

PUBS AND OTHER THATCHED BUSINESSES

In the 1950s, the people of Laois started to push away from traditional thatched dwellings in favour of more modern accommodation. But around that same time, publicans and the tourist industry began to capitalise on the traditional thatched roof as an attraction.

Tourists visiting Ireland were—and still are—charmed by the thought of having a pint in a cosy firelit room beneath a snug thatched roof. And despite the fact that they may no longer live in thatched houses, local people often like the fact that a family-run pub like Treacy's on the Heath has kept its thatch since 1780.

Michael Phelan's was a two-storey thatched public house and shop in the village of Donaghmore, near Rathdowney. It was purchased around 1909 by Michael Phelan, who ran the business with his wife, Delia. As well as being a publican, Mr Phelan was a farmer and a politician; he became an elected Sinn Féin member of Laois County Council in 1918. During the early 1960s, the public house section of the building (on the right of the photo), was knocked down and a new pub and dwelling for the family were built next door. The family continued to use the remaining portion of the original building for storage. In the early 1980s, its thatch was replaced by a slated roof.

Treacy's Bar and Restaurant

Treacy's Bar and Restaurant

Treacy's on the Heath is probably the only pub in Ireland that has been operated by the same family for eight generations. Although the thatched building has been dated to 1780, it may be older.

Tom Treacy, who was born in the house portion of the premises, began doing simple jobs in the pub, like sorting bottles, when he was five or six years old. "In those days, if you were part of the furniture, you were expected to help out," he explains. During his childhood, the pub bottled stout provided by Guinness. One of Tom's jobs was to paste on the labels that read: "Guinness, by Treacy's".

For many years, the public house included a shop. Then, in the early 1950s, Treacy's became an Esso service station and fuel pumps were added outside the pub. Twenty years later, both the grocery and service station businesses ceased, but around the same time the pub began to expand its food business.

Tom and his wife, Marie, took over the pub when his parents retired. They raised a daughter and four sons in the house portion of the building and lived there until 1997, when they built a new house nearby. At that time the domestic portion of the building was converted into additional kitchens to support Treacy's restaurant trade.

Tom Treacy belongs to the seventh generation of the Treacy family, which has owned and operated a pub on the Heath since 1780, and possibly earlier.

Today Treacy's clientele is fairly evenly split between locals and tourists. Because the Heath has no village centre, Treacy's has been a meeting place for the local people throughout its long history. It's also a centre for special occasions. First communions, confirmations and anniversaries are celebrated there, in addition to the everyday pub trade. Treacy's is also a gathering point for one of the big annual events in the county: the Gordon Bennett Race.

People interested in history and vernacular architecture are frequent visitors. "Thatched pubs have gone very scarce now, so having a thatched pub is very much a tourist attraction," Tom says. "Treacy's has become a landmark in the Midlands. People passing through the area will come just to have a look."

Two great thatchers maintained the roof at Treacy's for decades: Ted McEvoy and Sean Brennan. "Ted McEvoy was a great character who could turn his hand at anything," Tom says. "If Ted was in the pub having a drink, it wouldn't be long before he'd be surrounded by people who were listening to his stories. He was like a *seanchaí*."

The late Ted McEvoy

Mr Brennan, whom Tom describes as "one of the best thatchers of all time", was a highly talented Gaelic football player. Playing for the Heath and for Laois, he led teams to victory in five football championships during the late 1950s and early 1960s.

The Fisherman's Inn

Sean Ward bought the Fisherman's Inn in 1996 for a number of reasons, including that it reminded him a lot of his grandmother's house in Offaly. He has dated the building back to Cromwellian times, although it may well be older. It is built of field stone, mud and a few bricks, and a modern extension to the back gives the pub a T-shape.

This pub, located down a country road in Laois, has a worldwide following. In November 2010, the pub was full of American tourists one night and the focus of German travel writers the next. Ward found himself explaining the Irish wake and giving his recipe for Wake Tea on camera for a small television station out of Beijing, which reaches 22 million viewers.

The Fisherman's Inn also functions as a gathering place for the local community. Recently the Happy Snappers, an amateur camera club, staged an exhibition there. A local hunt group, complete with 150 horses (which stayed outside), stopped by before sounding their bugles and taking off down the road. Traditional music evenings are a regular event.

Ward's commitment to preserving this rare old building and maintaining its original thatched roof has been a shrewd business decision.

"Having a thatched pub is an attraction. For a pub out in the middle of nowhere we do okay. It's a busy pub. We'll get custom other pubs won't," he says.

SHEERAN'S PUB

When he was growing up in England, Kevin Hogan would often return to his mother's village of Coolrain to visit his grandparents. During those years, Sheeran's Pub was the social centre of the village. After he grew up and went into the public house business in England always, at the back of his mind, was the idea that if he were ever back in Ireland and Sheeran's pub came up for sale, he would buy it. "It wasn't a dream exactly," he says. "It's more that it was the place responsible for a lot of happy memories."

Before he purchased Sheeran's, it had been leased out for 12 years and had fallen into disrepair. At the time of this writing, he was working to put together financing to restore it, including returning the pub to its original roof of oaten straw. "It was always thatched with oaten straw," he says. "Now it's thatched with reed, but the plan is to go back to oaten straw because effectively that was what was used in the Midlands. It's more authentic. And from a personal preference, it looks nicer. You get that nice golden glow."

Most thatched pubs are country pubs or in rural areas and to keep them going you have to have ongoing help financially. Even when things were good, that type of pub would do their steady little trade and that was it. It's not as if the publicans made thousands of pounds, as they would in urban catchment areas. Ongoing help is very important. If you can get them to help you get the roof right…after that, of course it's your responsibility. It's not that dear to maintain if you get your thatcher back.

—KEVIN HOGAN

Bedroom of Fitzpatrick's Cottage

Self-Catering Holiday Homes

The holiday home industry has made much of vernacular thatched roofs. Entire websites are devoted to helping visitors to Ireland find thatched B&Bs or self-catering holiday houses. In Laois, Abbeyview Cottage in Jamestown, the Dowling family home near Emo and Fitzpatrick's Cottage near Clough offer visitors the chance to stay in rare, authentic Irish thatched houses.

Turning a thatched house into a self-catering holiday home is one way that owners have found to keep them financially viable. One such house is Fitzpatrick's Cottage near Clough, which is owned by Margaret and Patrick Brennan.

When the Brennans purchased the house, they worked with thatcher Jackie Kavanagh to restore the thatched roof. While working to maintain the best aspects of the traditional thatched house, the Brennans did make some improvements, such as installing a stove and converting Mrs Fitzpatrick's hen house and store into a bedroom.

Having a thatched roof is an asset, particularly when it comes to attracting foreign visitors, according to Margaret Brennan. Today Fitzpatrick's Cottage is featured on several websites for holiday makers who are interested in traditional homes.

Abbeyview Cottage, the family home of the Dempseys, is presently operated as a self-catering holiday home by Oliver Dempsey.

After his mother Ellen Dowling passed away, thatcher Jimmy Dowling completely renovated the thatched house that was the Dowling family home. Today he makes it available to visitors, including family members, as a self-catering holiday home.

THATCH IN A NEW ERA

Today, when so many counties in Ireland have lost their thatched dwellings, Laois is fortunate in that it still has 34 historic thatched houses. They have survived because a group of determined people realise that these houses are rare, precious and worth saving.

A number of people in the county have dedicated themselves to maintaining traditional thatched houses. Many do so because of strong family ties to a particular dwelling. Others believe that thatched houses are one of the best expressions of what makes Ireland itself. And finally, some people are attracted by the time-tested forms and sustainable, locally sourced materials that make a thatched house a harmonious part of the natural landscape.

Whatever their motivation, all owners of thatched houses apply themselves to the same basic issue: making thatched houses practical.

A 21st Century Thatch: Philip and Penny Doran's House

Value for money was the main reason Philip Doran and his wife Penny decided to buy and restore a traditional thatched house, rather than purchasing a new home back in 2001.

"We looked for a house for two years, but I just didn't feel there was any value in the new houses we could afford. And I didn't want to be tied down to a loan for years for something that wasn't worth the money," Philip explains. "Besides, we both liked old houses so we decided to restore an old house rather than buy new."

The house that they eventually purchased is one of three thatched houses in the area that appear on the 1911 Census. At that time, it was the home of a farmer named Patrick Loughlin, his wife, son and four daughters. It had lain empty for nearly a decade since the youngest of those daughters — Bridget Loughlin, who was listed on the Census as a two-year-old child — had passed away.

When the Dorans purchased the house, it had fallen into a derelict state. Briars were growing in the 1970s windows. A tumbledown building at one end, which had been a dairy, had lost its roof. Finally, the entire original thatched roof structure, including the roof beams, had been replaced with new wood and galvanised sheeting.

However, the house had one great asset: a well. "One of the reasons we bought here was that it had a good water supply. That made a huge difference to us. We had good drinking water and water to use during the building process," Philip says.

For the next six months, Philip and Penny worked together to make the house right again. "We're both good with our hands and we like to make things," explains Penny. "It was great fun working on the house together."

They began with the basics. "It was really a case of making it structurally sound again," Philip says. "We made good all the walls, windows and doors. The heads above the doors were rotten and every one of them had to be replaced. Once the walls were sound, we rewired the house. Then we replumbed it."

When it came to restoring the traditional parts of the house, such as the lime render and thatched roof, the Dorans did a lot of research. They talked to people who had worked on similar houses and read books on traditional building methods.

"You pick up a bit here and a bit there and you read stuff. Then you put your hands in and give it a go," says Penny. "If what you're doing goes wrong, you can usually figure out why right away."

Nearly everything that has gone into the restoration of Philip and Penny's house has been second-hand, reused or recycled. As the Dorans cleared the overgrown farmyard they discovered cobbles and flagstones they could use in flooring and paths around their property.

> *When we walked in through the front door, the house just wrapped itself around us and said: 'Welcome Home'.*
>
> — Penny Doran

They had a stroke of luck when a builder, who was a family friend, contacted them to say that he had just replaced the old sash windows of a farmhouse nearby and couldn't bear to throw them away. Could they use them?

There were enough sash windows to restore every window in the original house.

The most difficult part of the project was redoing the ceiling. One thing that made it a bit easier was the discovery of an immense metal pot that had been used to cook animal fodder. While they slaved away, the Dorans would heat four big kettles of water on the Stanley range. At the end of the day, they'd pour the kettles in the pot, top it up with a hose, and take turns having a soak. "It felt gorgeous at the time," Penny says.

When the Dorans decided to put the old thatched roof back, Philip chose to thatch the roof himself. After taking a course in thatching, he began to train with experienced thatchers in the county. Ultimately, the experience caused him to change careers and become a full-time thatcher.

The Dorans kept the original dimensions of the house, with one exception: they enlarged the doorway to a loft space so that Philip, who is six foot two, could use it more easily as an office.

Today the restored house is very comfortable. The insulation provided by its 20-inch-thick roof of oaten straw helps keep the house warm in the winter and cool in the summer. The tumbled down dairy has been converted into an en suite bathroom. Philip and Penny and their friends drink coffee and talk next to the stove beneath the original wooden lintel beam.

"Since we've moved here we've heard from local people that this was always a sociable house. Visitors and passing musicians would always find a meal and a bed here. It has always been a happy place," says Penny.

The Loughlins' house is now the Dorans' house. It is once again a welcoming family home.

There are so many factors in how a roof wears, including the shadow of trees, the quality of the straw or reed and the skill of the thatcher. In Laois we're landlocked; we don't have reed beds. Because of that, when I did my own house I wanted it done it in straw because I thought that would blend best into the entire landscape.

— PHILIP DORAN

Philip Doran

Philip Doran worked for several years as a software engineer in London. Then, in 1997 he and his wife Penny returned to Ireland, where they bought a ruined farmhouse and restored it, down to replacing the corrugated iron roof with the thatch roof that was original to the property.

Working with thatch was a revelation for Philip, who realised before long that being a thatcher was his calling. After taking some courses and training with other thatchers, including Seamus Conroy, he set up his own business in 2005. Today, he thatches in Laois, Offaly, Tipperary, Kildare and Kilkenny.

His philosophy about thatch is reflected in the motto on his van: "Heritage is part of the future".

In the past people thatched their houses because straw was cheap and available, Philip says, but today thatch has "green" credentials: it offers a locally sourced, sustainable, durable building material that gives a house exceptional insulation. He admits he was almost startled at how much more comfortable his own house became after he restored its thatched roof.

Replacing hard roofs with thatch gives him particular satisfaction: "The end result is a thing of beauty. It gives you pride to think you've put back a roof that's 100 years old," he says.

Hopefully, as more people build with environmental factors in mind, they will consider thatch, Philip says: "I'd like to see more new houses with thatched roofs."

Lesley Bailey's House

Although Lesley Bailey grew up in South County Dublin, she came to love the houses that belonged to rural Ireland during the long summers that her family spent in Wicklow. After raising three boys in Dublin, she bought her thatched house near Portarlington in 1995 and has lived there since.

"My house can be very cosy," she says. "When you get it heated, it's lovely and warm. When you're in there, you can't hear a thing outside. It's well built."

If you have any rural longing in you, a thatched house is where you find peace.

There's an idea of Ireland that has been over-commercialised; some people believe that you have to go all the way to Galway to find it. But when you see thatched cottages around the countryside, you have the feeling that you are in the real Ireland. You really feel the spirit of Ireland in a thatched house and you have to keep that feeling going.

—Lesley Bailey

CHALLENGES

Adapting traditional thatched houses and pubs to life in modern Ireland presents some challenges. A good place to start is by accepting that old houses do not function like new houses.

Understanding materials and the logic behind how they were used is essential to maintaining a traditional thatched house, according to Kay Moore.

"These houses were built in a way that suited the elements," she says. "For example, the damp passed through the walls, and if you put cement on the walls, although you might think you were protecting the wall, you'd actually be doing more damage than good."

One challenge some thatched house owners face is flooding. A house that was level with the road in 1700 when people were passing by on horseback may now be a foot below road level. Every time a road is resurfaced, it becomes a bit higher.

Many owners of thatched houses report a real problem with small birds picking at the straw. Philip Doran has found that placing a plastic magpie on the roof of the house scares away other birds.

Owners of thatched houses all agree that the grants for thatching and repairing thatch are inadequate. They come nowhere near the cost of putting on an entirely new thatched roof.

It can be difficult for owners to find good thatchers. And for thatchers themselves, the market is so small that making a living can be a challenge.

"We have to have more support for thatchers," says Sean Ward. "Thatching is an art and maybe the best thing would be for the government to recognise thatchers as artists and let them have tax free income."

Getting insurance for thatched dwellings is also a challenge. One owner of a thatched house—who would prefer not to be named—points out: "It is difficult to get insurance for thatched dwellings, even though many of them have survived for 300 years."

Other challenges facing owners include sourcing thatching materials, knowing how to apply for grants and covering the cost of the work. Many owners also worry about the future of their homes and whether the next generation will be interested in looking after the thatch.

Some of these challenges could be overcome by establishing a network or community of thatch owners in County Laois. Through this network owners could help each other by sharing information about grants and insurance and thatchers could meet the owners easily and offer their services.

Opposite page: A few months before he passed away, Ned Ging harvested oats to thatch the house in which he had lived his entire life.

THE LAST WORD

I'd hate to see a modern house here. I keep this house because it's part of the farm. It just suits the place.

—Bridie Lewis

It's an overcast October day in the heart of Laois. Ducks chase each other through the low mist on the ponds, and every blade of grass seems wrapped in gray cotton wool.

But down a laneway there is a sudden blaze of gold. One side of an L-shaped farmhouse is covered with a shaggy coat of oaten straw. On the other side, two lads stand on a scaffold. Usually they install insulation for a living but today, under the careful supervision of 82-year-old Ned Ging, who has been thatching this house for most of his life, they are learning a new skill. Except, of course, it's an ancient skill, one that has been practiced for as long as farmers have grown grain.

One lad hands up hairpin scollops; the other uses a mallet to hammer them into the bundles of straw already placed on the roof. Meanwhile the boys' father pares additional scollops in the barn.

Bridie Lewis looks on. For her, the periodic thatching of the house is one of the natural rhythms of life on the farm, like the hatching out of chicks in the spring or harvesting beetroot in the autumn. She intends to maintain the thatched roof for as long as she's able.

ABOUT THE AUTHORS

Mary Ann Williams is a writer and editor who specialises in heritage and natural history. Her past clients include the Field Museum of Natural History in Chicago; the Monterey Bay Aquarium in Monterey, California; the County Museum, Dundalk; St Patrick's Cathedral, Dublin; and the Heritage Officers of Counties Laois, Offaly and Sligo.

Mary Ann is also the leader of the 20th Dublin Beaver Scouts. She lives in Dublin with her husband and two children, whose support has been invaluable during the writing of this book.

Bronagh Lanigan is a History of Art graduate of University College Dublin and has completed two post-graduate diplomas in Architectural Inventory and Recording (DIT, Bolton Street) and Applied Building Repair and Conservation (Trinity College Dublin).

Bronagh has long had an interest in historic buildings and having worked on inventories of thatched buildings in County Laois and South Tipperary County, has developed a keen interest and understanding of vernacular thatched structures.

Sinéad Hughes is an Archaeology graduate of University College Dublin and has completed two post-graduate diplomas in Architectural Inventory and Recording (DIT, Bolton Street) and Applied Building Repair and Conservation (Trinity College Dublin).

As an Architectural Heritage Consultant, Sinéad has recorded and carried out research into many post-1700 buildings throughout Ireland. She has developed a particular appreciation for Ireland's vernacular buildings and their unique stories.

Architectural Recording and Research (AR&R) is an architectural heritage consultancy which provides conservation and research services to a variety of clients. Established by Bronagh Lanigan and Sinéad Hughes in 2001, AR&R specialises in large and small-scale inventories and architectural heritage reports. In 2007, AR&R carried out the *Survey of Thatched Structures of County Laois* for Laois County Council. For more information about AR&R, see www.arr.ie.

BIBLIOGRAPHY

Danaher, Kevin. *Ireland's Vernacular Architecture*, Second Edition, The Government of Ireland, Dublin, 1978.

Fitzsimons, Jack. *Bungalow Bliss*, Kells Art Studios, Kells, County Meath, 1976.

Kinmonth, Claudia, *Irish Rural Interiors in Art*, Yale University Press, New Haven and London, 2006.

O'Keeffe, Maurice. Interview with Seamus Conroy, Graigueafulla, Clonaslee, June 2006. Laois-Offaly Collection, CD 39. Irish Life & Lore Series, www.irishlifeandlore.com.

O'Neill, Timothy. *Life and Tradition in Rural Ireland*, J.M. Dent and Sons, Ltd., 1977.

O'Reilly, Barry. *Living Under Thatch: Vernacular Architecture in County Offaly*, Mercier Press, Cork, 2004.

PHOTO INDEX

Cover
    Oats being grown to thatch Ned Ging's house near Portlaoise

Inside front cover
    Ned Ging's roof during thatching

Table of Contents
    Entrance to Liam McEvoy's house near Mountmellick

p 4   Jimmy Dowling's ladder

p 5   Hanging basket at Thatched House, Morette, Emo

p 6   Ripening oats, early summer

p 7   Freshly thatched roof, near Emo

p 8   Household and Building returns for Bates Family from the 1911 Census

p 9   Detail from 1911 Census documents
    Archival image of a house on the Heath, courtesy of Jackie Hyland

p 10 Mary Ann Bergin outside Bergin's house, Ballytarsna, Pike of Rushall in the late 1950s, courtesy of Tony Bergin

p 11 Inside the Dunne family house at Clonaghadoo

p 12 The Poet's Cottage near Camross
    Detail of straight scollops held in place by hairpin scollops
    Ridge by Philip Doran

p 13 Jimmy Dowling at work

p 14 Súgán rope holding layers of scraw to rafters of The Fisherman's Inn
    Roof structure and pictures in the Dunne family's house at Clonaghadoo

p 15 Scraw above rafters, courtesy of Jackie Hyland
    Hipped roof on Noel Butler's house near Rosenallis

p 16 Súgán rope being made
    Scollops and mallet
    Michael Dempsey positions a bundle of fresh thatch
    Jimmy Dowling at work near Emo

p 17 Roof finial with copper top by Michael Dempsey
    Ridge detail by Philip Doran
    Michael Dempsey uses a mallet to secure a straight scollop that will hold a ridge of bobbins in place

p 18 Family portrait courtesy of Kenneth Keogh
    Three whitewashed walls
    John O'Rourke Jnr, Kenneth Keogh, Mary O'Rourke, John O Rourke Snr and James Keogh standing in front of Sean Costello's pub in Killenard, Portarlington in 1972, courtesy of Kenneth Keogh

p 19 Doorway of Dunne family home at Clonaghadoo
    Doorway of out-building on Bridie Lewis's farm near Portlaoise
    Side wall of Abbeyview Cottage near Ballybrittas
    Kitchen of Bridie Lewis's farmhouse near Portlaoise

p 20 Hearth with canopy at Dunne family home at Clonaghadoo

p 22 Shutter detail from The Fisherman's Inn, Fisherstown
    Thatched house floorplans (Máirtín D'Alton)

p 23 Houseleek growing on wall of thatched house
    Liam and Abigail McEvoy's thatched house near Mountmellick

p 24 & 25 Abbeyview Cottage near Ballybrittas

p 26 Michael Dempsey

p 27 Michael Dempsey uses hairpin and straight scollops to secure fresh thatch
    A mallet on top of a roof of old thatch
    Michael and Martin Dempsey make súgán rope near Ballybrittas

p 28 Ripe oats ready for harvest near Portlaoise
    Harvesting oats for thatching near Portlaoise

p 29 Oat stooks near Portlaoise
    Friends and neighbours thresh oats for thatching Ned Ging's house, including Matt, Jackie and Andy Hyland, Luke Tynan, James and Seamus McGrath, Brian Lewis, Des Thornton, Liam and Louis Troy, Ned Ging and Jim Hyland
    Detail of threshing mill

p 30 Freshly trimmed hazel scollops
    Hairpin scollop
    Philip Doran's tools

p 31 The Fisherman's Inn, Fisherstown
    Reed thatch over window of Nancy Phelan's House, near Cullahill
    Green oats

p 32 Thatched houses at Cullahill (top), The Waterfall near Vicarstown (middle) and Newtown near Durrow (Máirtín D'Alton)

p 33 The Dowling family in front of their thatched house near Emo, courtesy of Meaghan Dowling

p 34 Nancy Phelan outside her house near Cullahill

p 35 Theresa Delahunty in her thatched house near Durrow

p 36 Jimmy Dowling and Dowling family photo

p 37 Hyland family home on the Heath, Portlaoise, courtesy of Maria Hyland
    Sheila, Noel (in the doorway), Joe and Sarah Bergin, as well as an unidentified lady (in hat), with Nelson the dog in front of the Bergin family home, Ballytarsna, Pike of Rushall, during the early 1960s, courtesy of Tony Bergin
    Eileen Keogh and Junia Root with Rover the dog outside the Keogh family home in Huntington, Portarlington in 1964 (Larry Carroll cutting the hedge in the background), courtesy of Kenneth Keogh
    Lesley Bailey's house in the snow in 2009, courtesy of Lesley Bailey

p 38 Lil, Lena, Tom and Madge (Margaret) McLoughlin circa 1945
    Margaret McLoughlin Mulhall in front of her family home at Jamestown Cross near Ballybrittas

p 39 Thatched House at Jamestown Cross
    Door detail of house at Jamestown Cross
    Thomas McLoughlin Snr circa 1945
    Tom McLoughlin Jnr circa 1990

p 40 Window sill in Crannagh House
    Crannagh House near Stradbally

p 41 Kay Moore with a self-portrait of her grandmother, Emily Lynch Williams
    Crannagh House before and after thatching by Seamus Conroy
    Ivor and Seamus Conroy

p 42 Eddie and Edward Dunne in doorway of Dunne family home at Clonaghadoo
    The Dunne family home at Clonaghadoo

p 43 Pump, hearth and dresser from the house at Clonaghadoo

p 44 Refrigerator and laundry ads courtesy of the ESB archive
    Electric cooking article, circa 1963, courtesy of *Woman's Way* magazine

P 45 ESB iron and kettle ads courtesy of the ESB Archive
    Mrs B iron ad courtesy of Stork Margarine
    Lamp from the house at Clonaghadoo

p 46 Mary Bergin in the doorway of the house in which she was born near Ballacolla
    Detail of gate from Mary Bergin's house
    Mary Bergin's dog inside her thatched house near Ballacolla
    Cowboy ad, courtesy of the ESB Archive

p 47 A grandchild outside Mary Bergin's House near Ballacolla
    Jackie Kavanagh's thatched house near Ballacolla (Máirtín D'Alton)

p 48 Cover of 1976 edition of *Bungalow Bliss*
    Tom Lawlor's family home, courtesy of Tom Lawlor

p 49 Archival photo of derelict cottage on the Heath, near Portlaoise, courtesy of Jackie Hyland

p 50 Michael Phelan's thatched pub and shop in Donaghmore, courtesy of Gertie Keane
    Treacy's Thatched Pub, the Heath near Portlaoise

p 51 Tom Treacy
    Ted McEvoy (RIP) rethatching Treacy's Pub, courtesy of Tom Treacy

p 52 Sean and Elizabeth Ward with their grandson John Henry in front of The Fisherman's Inn
    Window seat in The Fisherman's Inn
    Doorway at The Fisherman's Inn

p 53 Kevin Hogan, owner of Sheeran's Pub in Coolrain
    Fireplace in Sheeran's Pub, Coolrain
    Interior of Sheeran's Pub
    Sheeran's Pub, Coolrain

p 54 Bedroom at Fitzpatrick's Cottage, Clough
    Abbeyview Cottage, Ballybrittas
    Fitzpatrick's Cottage, Clough
    Morette Cottage, Emo

p 55 Thatched house near Ballacolla

p 56 Ridge detail from Philip Doran's house, near Rathdowney
    Window of Philip Doran's house
    Philip Doran sharpening a scollop

p 57 Philip and Penny Doran's house near Rathdowney

p 58 Ladder leading to Philip Doran's office
    Philip and Penny Doran in their living room

p 59 Philip Doran and his tools
    Lesley Bailey's house near Portarlington

p 60 Ned Ging RIP carrying oats grown to thatch his house near Portlaoise

p 61 Plastic decoy magpies on Philip Doran's house near Rathdowney

p 62 Alan, Declan and Ronan O'Brien thatching Ned Ging's house near Portlaoise

p 64 Hens on Bridie Lewis's farm near Portlaoise

p 65 Montage of images from the thatched houses of Laois by James Fraher

Back cover
    Apple tree outside Abbeyview Cottage near Ballybrittas

Thatched houses look so well in the countryside. Golden. They'd be shining now in good weather like this.

—SEAMUS CONROY